ASA-SP-FLT-2

THE STANDARD® AIRCRAFT FLIGHT LOG
SP-FLT-2

ASA-SP-FLT-2
ISBN 978-1-56027-761-3

Published by
Aviation Supplies & Academics, Inc.
7005 132nd Place SE
Newcastle, WA 98059-3153
Website: www.asa2fly.com
Email: asa@asa2fly.com

Printed in the United States of America

[19] 22

TRANSPORTATION USD $15.95

ISBN 978-1-56027-761-3

51595 >

9 781560 277613

Aircraft Flight Log

Aircraft

N-Number ______________________________

Type ______________________________

Serial Number ______________________________

Engine Serial Number(s) ______________________________

____

Date of Purchase ______________________________

Owner

Name ______________________________

Telephone ______________________________

Address ______________________________

City, State ______________________________

Zip ______________________________

Email ______________________________

Book

Number ______________________________

From Date/Tach ______________________________

To Date/Tach ______________________________

Date 20___	Pilot	Time			Destination/ Purpose
		Out	In	Total	

Total______

Squawks/ Inspections	Ok'd By	Date	Oil Added

Oil Change

Due:___________

100-hour

Due:___________

Annual

Due:___________

VOR check

Due:___________

Due:___________

Due:___________

Pitot-Static check

Due:___________

ELT check

Due:___________

GPS Database

Due:___________

Instructions: Describe any squawk affecting flight. Record the inspections you perform, including the pitot static system, transponder, ELT, ELT battery, VOR test, and GPS database updates (verify database cycle No. on the startup screen).

Date 20____	Pilot	Time			Destination/ Purpose
		Out	In	Total	

Total______

Squawks/ Inspections	Ok'd By	Date	Oil Added

Oil Change

Due:__________

100-hour

Due:__________

Annual

Due:__________

VOR check

Due:__________

Due:__________

Due:__________

Pitot-Static check

Due:__________

ELT check

Due:__________

GPS Database

Due:__________

Instructions: Describe any squawk affecting flight. Record the inspections you perform, including the pitot static system, transponder, ELT, ELT battery, VOR test, and GPS database updates (verify database cycle No. on the startup screen).

Date 20___	Pilot	Time			Destination/ Purpose
		Out	In	Total	

Total______

Squawks/ Inspections	Ok'd By	Date	Oil Added

Oil Change

Due:____________

100-hour

Due:____________

Annual

Due:____________

VOR check

Due:____________

Due:____________

Due:____________

Pitot-Static check

Due:____________

ELT check

Due:____________

GPS Database

Due:____________

Instructions: Describe any squawk affecting flight. Record the inspections you perform, including the pitot static system, transponder, ELT, ELT battery, VOR test, and GPS database updates (verify database cycle No. on the startup screen).

Date 20___	Pilot	Time			Destination/ Purpose
		Out	In	Total	

Total______

Squawks/ Inspections	Ok'd By	Date	Oil Added

Oil Change

Due:___________

100-hour

Due:___________

Annual

Due:___________

VOR check

Due:___________

Due:___________

Due:___________

Pitot-Static check

Due:___________

ELT check

Due:___________

GPS Database

Due:___________

Instructions: Describe any squawk affecting flight. Record the inspections you perform, including the pitot static system, transponder, ELT, ELT battery, VOR test, and GPS database updates (verify database cycle No. on the startup screen).

Date 20___	Pilot	Time			Destination/ Purpose
		Out	In	Total	

Total______

Squawks/ Inspections	Ok'd By	Date	Oil Added

Oil Change

Due:____________

100-hour

Due:____________

Annual

Due:____________

VOR check

Due:____________

Due:____________

Due:____________

Pitot-Static check

Due:____________

ELT check

Due:____________

GPS Database

Due:____________

Instructions: Describe any squawk affecting flight. Record the inspections you perform, including the pitot static system, transponder, ELT, ELT battery, VOR test, and GPS database updates (verify database cycle No. on the startup screen).

Date 20____	Pilot	Time			Destination/ Purpose
		Out	In	Total	

Total______

Squawks/ Inspections	Ok'd By	Date	Oil Added

Oil Change

Due:____________

100-hour

Due:____________

Annual

Due:____________

VOR check

Due:____________

Due:____________

Due:____________

Pitot-Static check

Due:____________

ELT check

Due:____________

GPS Database

Due:____________

Instructions: Describe any squawk affecting flight. Record the inspections you perform, including the pitot static system, transponder, ELT, ELT battery, VOR test, and GPS database updates (verify database cycle No. on the startup screen).

Date 20___	Pilot	Time			Destination/ Purpose
		Out	In	Total	

Total______

Squawks/ Inspections	Ok'd By	Date	Oil Added

Oil Change

Due:___________

100-hour

Due:___________

Annual

Due:___________

VOR check

Due:___________

Due:___________

Due:___________

Pitot-Static check

Due:___________

ELT check

Due:___________

GPS Database

Due:___________

Instructions: Describe any squawk affecting flight. Record the inspections you perform, including the pitot static system, transponder, ELT, ELT battery, VOR test, and GPS database updates (verify database cycle No. on the startup screen).

Date 20___	Pilot	Time			Destination/ Purpose
		Out	In	Total	

Total______

Squawks/ Inspections	Ok'd By	Date	Oil Added

Oil Change

Due:____________

100-hour

Due:____________

Annual

Due:____________

VOR check

Due:____________

Due:____________

Due:____________

Pitot-Static check

Due:____________

ELT check

Due:____________

GPS Database

Due:____________

Instructions: Describe any squawk affecting flight. Record the inspections you perform, including the pitot static system, transponder, ELT, ELT battery, VOR test, and GPS database updates (verify database cycle No. on the startup screen).

Date 20___	Pilot	Time			Destination/ Purpose
		Out	In	Total	

Total______

Squawks/ Inspections	Ok'd By	Date	Oil Added

Oil Change

Due:____________

100-hour

Due:____________

Annual

Due:____________

VOR check

Due:____________

Due:____________

Due:____________

Pitot-Static check

Due:____________

ELT check

Due:____________

GPS Database

Due:____________

Instructions: Describe any squawk affecting flight. Record the inspections you perform, including the pitot static system, transponder, ELT, ELT battery, VOR test, and GPS database updates (verify database cycle No. on the startup screen).

Date 20___	Pilot	Time			Destination/ Purpose
		Out	In	Total	

Total______

Squawks/ Inspections	Ok'd By	Date	Oil Added

Oil Change

Due:____________

100-hour

Due:____________

Annual

Due:____________

VOR check

Due:____________

Due:____________

Due:____________

Pitot-Static check

Due:____________

ELT check

Due:____________

GPS Database

Due:____________

Instructions: Describe any squawk affecting flight. Record the inspections you perform, including the pitot static system, transponder, ELT, ELT battery, VOR test, and GPS database updates (verify database cycle No. on the startup screen).

Date 20___	Pilot	Time			Destination/ Purpose
		Out	In	Total	

Total______

Squawks/ Inspections	Ok'd By	Date	Oil Added

Oil Change

Due:____________

100-hour

Due:____________

Annual

Due:____________

VOR check

Due:____________

Due:____________

Due:____________

Pitot-Static check

Due:____________

ELT check

Due:____________

GPS Database

Due:____________

Instructions: Describe any squawk affecting flight. Record the inspections you perform, including the pitot static system, transponder, ELT, ELT battery, VOR test, and GPS database updates (verify database cycle No. on the startup screen).

Date 20___	Pilot	Time			Destination/ Purpose
		Out	In	Total	

Total______

Squawks/ Inspections	Ok'd By	Date	Oil Added

Oil Change

Due:____________

100-hour

Due:____________

Annual

Due:____________

VOR check

Due:____________

Due:____________

Due:____________

Pitot-Static check

Due:____________

ELT check

Due:____________

GPS Database

Due:____________

Instructions: Describe any squawk affecting flight. Record the inspections you perform, including the pitot static system, transponder, ELT, ELT battery, VOR test, and GPS database updates (verify database cycle No. on the startup screen).

Date 20___	Pilot	Time			Destination/ Purpose
		Out	In	Total	

Total______

Squawks/ Inspections	Ok'd By	Date	Oil Added

Oil Change

Due:__________

100-hour

Due:__________

Annual

Due:__________

VOR check

Due:__________

Due:__________

Due:__________

Pitot-Static check

Due:__________

ELT check

Due:__________

GPS Database

Due:__________

Instructions: Describe any squawk affecting flight. Record the inspections you perform, including the pitot static system, transponder, ELT, ELT battery, VOR test, and GPS database updates (verify database cycle No. on the startup screen).

Date 20____	Pilot	Time			Destination/ Purpose
		Out	In	Total	

Total______

Squawks/ Inspections	Ok'd By	Date	Oil Added

Oil Change

Due:__________

100-hour

Due:__________

Annual

Due:__________

VOR check

Due:__________

Due:__________

Due:__________

Pitot-Static check

Due:__________

ELT check

Due:__________

GPS Database

Due:__________

Instructions: Describe any squawk affecting flight. Record the inspections you perform, including the pitot static system, transponder, ELT, ELT battery, VOR test, and GPS database updates (verify database cycle No. on the startup screen).

Date 20___	Pilot	Time			Destination/ Purpose
		Out	In	Total	

Total______

Squawks/ Inspections	**Ok'd By**	**Date**	**Oil Added**

Oil Change

Due:___________

100-hour

Due:___________

Annual

Due:___________

VOR check

Due:___________

Due:___________

Due:___________

Pitot-Static check

Due:___________

ELT check

Due:___________

GPS Database

Due:___________

Instructions: Describe any squawk affecting flight. Record the inspections you perform, including the pitot static system, transponder, ELT, ELT battery, VOR test, and GPS database updates (verify database cycle No. on the startup screen).

Date 20____	Pilot	Time			Destination/ Purpose
		Out	In	Total	

Total______

Squawks/ Inspections	Ok'd By	Date	Oil Added

Oil Change

Due:__________

100-hour

Due:__________

Annual

Due:__________

VOR check

Due:__________

Due:__________

Due:__________

Pitot-Static check

Due:__________

ELT check

Due:__________

GPS Database

Due:__________

Instructions: Describe any squawk affecting flight. Record the inspections you perform, including the pitot static system, transponder, ELT, ELT battery, VOR test, and GPS database updates (verify database cycle No. on the startup screen).

Date 20____	Pilot	Time			Destination/ Purpose
		Out	In	Total	

Total______

Squawks/ Inspections	Ok'd By	Date	Oil Added

Oil Change

Due:___________

100-hour

Due:___________

Annual

Due:___________

VOR check

Due:___________

Due:___________

Due:___________

Pitot-Static check

Due:___________

ELT check

Due:___________

GPS Database

Due:___________

Instructions: Describe any squawk affecting flight. Record the inspections you perform, including the pitot static system, transponder, ELT, ELT battery, VOR test, and GPS database updates (verify database cycle No. on the startup screen).

Date 20___	Pilot	Time			Destination/ Purpose
		Out	In	Total	

Total______

Squawks/ Inspections	**Ok'd By**	**Date**	**Oil Added**

Oil Change

Due:___________

100-hour

Due:___________

Annual

Due:___________

VOR check

Due:___________

Due:___________

Due:___________

Pitot-Static check

Due:___________

ELT check

Due:___________

GPS Database

Due:___________

Instructions: Describe any squawk affecting flight. Record the inspections you perform, including the pitot static system, transponder, ELT, ELT battery, VOR test, and GPS database updates (verify database cycle No. on the startup screen).

Date 20___	Pilot	Time			Destination/ Purpose
		Out	In	Total	

Total______

Squawks/ Inspections	Ok'd By	Date	Oil Added

Oil Change

Due:__________

100-hour

Due:__________

Annual

Due:__________

VOR check

Due:__________

Due:__________

Due:__________

Pitot-Static check

Due:__________

ELT check

Due:__________

GPS Database

Due:__________

Instructions: Describe any squawk affecting flight. Record the inspections you perform, including the pitot static system, transponder, ELT, ELT battery, VOR test, and GPS database updates (verify database cycle No. on the startup screen).

Date 20___	Pilot	Time			Destination/ Purpose
		Out	In	Total	

Total______

Squawks/ Inspections	Ok'd By	Date	Oil Added

Oil Change

Due:____________

100-hour

Due:____________

Annual

Due:____________

VOR check

Due:____________

Due:____________

Due:____________

Pitot-Static check

Due:____________

ELT check

Due:____________

GPS Database

Due:____________

Instructions: Describe any squawk affecting flight. Record the inspections you perform, including the pitot static system, transponder, ELT, ELT battery, VOR test, and GPS database updates (verify database cycle No. on the startup screen).

Date 20___	Pilot	Time			Destination/ Purpose
		Out	In	Total	

Total______

Squawks/ Inspections	Ok'd By	Date	Oil Added

Oil Change

Due:____________

100-hour

Due:____________

Annual

Due:____________

VOR check

Due:____________

Due:____________

Due:____________

Pitot-Static check

Due:____________

ELT check

Due:____________

GPS Database

Due:____________

Instructions: Describe any squawk affecting flight. Record the inspections you perform, including the pitot static system, transponder, ELT, ELT battery, VOR test, and GPS database updates (verify database cycle No. on the startup screen).

Date 20___	Pilot	Time			Destination/ Purpose
		Out	In	Total	

Total______

Squawks/ Inspections	Ok'd By	Date	Oil Added

Oil Change

Due:____________

100-hour

Due:____________

Annual

Due:____________

VOR check

Due:____________

Due:____________

Due:____________

Pitot-Static check

Due:____________

ELT check

Due:____________

GPS Database

Due:____________

Instructions: Describe any squawk affecting flight. Record the inspections you perform, including the pitot static system, transponder, ELT, ELT battery, VOR test, and GPS database updates (verify database cycle No. on the startup screen).

Date 20____	Pilot	Time			Destination/ Purpose
		Out	In	Total	

Total______

Squawks/ Inspections	Ok'd By	Date	Oil Added

Oil Change

Due:____________

100-hour

Due:____________

Annual

Due:____________

VOR check

Due:____________

Due:____________

Due:____________

Pitot-Static check

Due:____________

ELT check

Due:____________

GPS Database

Due:____________

Instructions: Describe any squawk affecting flight. Record the inspections you perform, including the pitot static system, transponder, ELT, ELT battery, VOR test, and GPS database updates (verify database cycle No. on the startup screen).

Date 20___	Pilot	Time			Destination/ Purpose
		Out	In	Total	

Total______

Squawks/ Inspections	Ok'd By	Date	Oil Added

Oil Change

Due:____________

100-hour

Due:____________

Annual

Due:____________

VOR check

Due:____________

Due:____________

Due:____________

Pitot-Static check

Due:____________

ELT check

Due:____________

GPS Database

Due:____________

Instructions: Describe any squawk affecting flight. Record the inspections you perform, including the pitot static system, transponder, ELT, ELT battery, VOR test, and GPS database updates (verify database cycle No. on the startup screen).

Date 20____	Pilot	Time			Destination/ Purpose
		Out	In	Total	

Total______

Squawks/ Inspections	Ok'd By	Date	Oil Added

Oil Change

Due:__________

100-hour

Due:__________

Annual

Due:__________

VOR check

Due:__________

Due:__________

Due:__________

Pitot-Static check

Due:__________

ELT check

Due:__________

GPS Database

Due:__________

Instructions: Describe any squawk affecting flight. Record the inspections you perform, including the pitot static system, transponder, ELT, ELT battery, VOR test, and GPS database updates (verify database cycle No. on the startup screen).

Date 20___	Pilot	Time			Destination/ Purpose
		Out	In	Total	

Total______

Squawks/ Inspections	Ok'd By	Date	Oil Added

Oil Change

Due:___________

100-hour

Due:___________

Annual

Due:___________

VOR check

Due:___________

Due:___________

Due:___________

Pitot-Static check

Due:_______

ELT check

Due:___________

GPS Database

Due:___________

Instructions: Describe any squawk affecting flight. Record the inspections you perform, including the pitot static system, transponder, ELT, ELT battery, VOR test, and GPS database updates (verify database cycle No. on the startup screen).

Date 20___	Pilot	Time			Destination/ Purpose
		Out	In	Total	

Total______

Squawks/ Inspections	Ok'd By	Date	Oil Added

Oil Change

Due:____________

100-hour

Due:____________

Annual

Due:____________

VOR check

Due:____________

Due:____________

Due:____________

Pitot-Static check

Due:____________

ELT check

Due:____________

GPS Database

Due:____________

Instructions: Describe any squawk affecting flight. Record the inspections you perform, including the pitot static system, transponder, ELT, ELT battery, VOR test, and GPS database updates (verify database cycle No. on the startup screen).

Date 20___	Pilot	Time			Destination/ Purpose
		Out	In	Total	

Total______

Squawks/ Inspections	Ok'd By	Date	Oil Added

Oil Change

Due:____________

100-hour

Due:____________

Annual

Due:____________

VOR check

Due:____________

Due:____________

Due:____________

Pitot-Static check

Due:____________

ELT check

Due:____________

GPS Database

Due:____________

Instructions: Describe any squawk affecting flight. Record the inspections you perform, including the pitot static system, transponder, ELT, ELT battery, VOR test, and GPS database updates (verify database cycle No. on the startup screen).

Date 20___	Pilot	Time			Destination/ Purpose
		Out	In	Total	

Total______

Squawks/ Inspections	Ok'd By	Date	Oil Added

Oil Change

Due:__________

100-hour

Due:__________

Annual

Due:__________

VOR check

Due:__________

Due:__________

Due:__________

Pitot-Static check

Due:__________

ELT check

Due:__________

GPS Database

Due:__________

Instructions: Describe any squawk affecting flight. Record the inspections you perform, including the pitot static system, transponder, ELT, ELT battery, VOR test, and GPS database updates (verify database cycle No. on the startup screen).

Date 20____	Pilot	Time			Destination/ Purpose
		Out	In	Total	

Total______

Squawks/ Inspections	Ok'd By	Date	Oil Added

Oil Change

Due:____________

100-hour

Due:____________

Annual

Due:____________

VOR check

Due:____________

Due:____________

Due:____________

Pitot-Static check

Due:____________

ELT check

Due:____________

GPS Database

Due:____________

Instructions: Describe any squawk affecting flight. Record the inspections you perform, including the pitot static system, transponder, ELT, ELT battery, VOR test, and GPS database updates (verify database cycle No. on the startup screen).

Date 20___	Pilot	Time			Destination/ Purpose
		Out	In	Total	

Total______

Squawks/ Inspections	Ok'd By	Date	Oil Added

Oil Change

Due:____________

100-hour

Due:____________

Annual

Due:____________

VOR check

Due:____________

Due:____________

Due:____________

Pitot-Static check

Due:____________

ELT check

Due:____________

GPS Database

Due:____________

Instructions: Describe any squawk affecting flight. Record the inspections you perform, including the pitot static system, transponder, ELT, ELT battery, VOR test, and GPS database updates (verify database cycle No. on the startup screen).

Date 20___	Pilot	Time			Destination/ Purpose
		Out	In	Total	

Total______

Squawks/ Inspections	Ok'd By	Date	Oil Added

Oil Change

Due:____________

100-hour

Due:____________

Annual

Due:____________

VOR check

Due:____________

Due:____________

Due:____________

Pitot-Static check

Due:____________

ELT check

Due:____________

GPS Database

Due:____________

Instructions: Describe any squawk affecting flight. Record the inspections you perform, including the pitot static system, transponder, ELT, ELT battery, VOR test, and GPS database updates (verify database cycle No. on the startup screen).

Date 20___	Pilot	Time			Destination/ Purpose
		Out	In	Total	

Total______

Squawks/ Inspections	Ok'd By	Date	Oil Added

Oil Change

Due:____________

100-hour

Due:____________

Annual

Due:____________

VOR check

Due:____________

Due:____________

Due:____________

Pitot-Static check

Due:____________

ELT check

Due:____________

GPS Database

Due:____________

Instructions: Describe any squawk affecting flight. Record the inspections you perform, including the pitot static system, transponder, ELT, ELT battery, VOR test, and GPS database updates (verify database cycle No. on the startup screen).

Date 20___	Pilot	Time			Destination/ Purpose
		Out	In	Total	

Total______

Squawks/ Inspections	Ok'd By	Date	Oil Added

Oil Change

Due:____________

100-hour

Due:____________

Annual

Due:____________

VOR check

Due:____________

Due:____________

Due:____________

Pitot-Static check

Due:____________

ELT check

Due:____________

GPS Database

Due:____________

Instructions: Describe any squawk affecting flight. Record the inspections you perform, including the pitot static system, transponder, ELT, ELT battery, VOR test, and GPS database updates (verify database cycle No. on the startup screen).

Date 20___	Pilot	Time			Destination/ Purpose
		Out	In	Total	

Total______

Squawks/ Inspections	Ok'd By	Date	Oil Added

Oil Change

Due:__________

100-hour

Due:__________

Annual

Due:__________

VOR check

Due:__________

Due:__________

Due:__________

Pitot-Static check

Due:__________

ELT check

Due:__________

GPS Database

Due:__________

Instructions: Describe any squawk affecting flight. Record the inspections you perform, including the pitot static system, transponder, ELT, ELT battery, VOR test, and GPS database updates (verify database cycle No. on the startup screen).

Date 20___	Pilot	Time			Destination/ Purpose
		Out	In	Total	

Total______

Squawks/ Inspections	Ok'd By	Date	Oil Added

Oil Change

Due:____________

100-hour

Due:____________

Annual

Due:____________

VOR check

Due:____________

Due:____________

Due:____________

Pitot-Static check

Due:____________

ELT check

Due:____________

GPS Database

Due:____________

Instructions: Describe any squawk affecting flight. Record the inspections you perform, including the pitot static system, transponder, ELT, ELT battery, VOR test, and GPS database updates (verify database cycle No. on the startup screen).

Date 20___	Pilot	Time			Destination/ Purpose
		Out	In	Total	

Total______

Squawks/ Inspections	Ok'd By	Date	Oil Added

Oil Change

Due:____________

100-hour

Due:____________

Annual

Due:____________

VOR check

Due:____________

Due:____________

Due:____________

Pitot-Static check

Due:____________

ELT check

Due:____________

GPS Database

Due:____________

Instructions: Describe any squawk affecting flight. Record the inspections you perform, including the pitot static system, transponder, ELT, ELT battery, VOR test, and GPS database updates (verify database cycle No. on the startup screen).

Date 20___	Pilot	Time			Destination/ Purpose
		Out	In	Total	

Total______

Squawks/ Inspections	Ok'd By	Date	Oil Added

Oil Change

Due:____________

100-hour

Due:____________

Annual

Due:____________

VOR check

Due:____________

Due:____________

Due:____________

Pitot-Static check

Due:____________

ELT check

Due:____________

GPS Database

Due:____________

Instructions: Describe any squawk affecting flight. Record the inspections you perform, including the pitot static system, transponder, ELT, ELT battery, VOR test, and GPS database updates (verify database cycle No. on the startup screen).

Date 20___	Pilot	Time			Destination/ Purpose
		Out	In	Total	

Total______

Squawks/ Inspections	Ok'd By	Date	Oil Added

Oil Change

Due:____________

100-hour

Due:____________

Annual

Due:____________

VOR check

Due:____________

Due:____________

Due:____________

Pitot-Static check

Due:____________

ELT check

Due:____________

GPS Database

Due:____________

Instructions: Describe any squawk affecting flight. Record the inspections you perform, including the pitot static system, transponder, ELT, ELT battery, VOR test, and GPS database updates (verify database cycle No. on the startup screen).

Date 20___	Pilot	Time			Destination/ Purpose
		Out	In	Total	

Total______

Squawks/ Inspections	**Ok'd By**	**Date**	**Oil Added**

Oil Change

Due:____________

100-hour

Due:____________

Annual

Due:____________

VOR check

Due:____________

Due:____________

Due:____________

Pitot-Static check

Due:____________

ELT check

Due:____________

GPS Database

Due:____________

Instructions: Describe any squawk affecting flight. Record the inspections you perform, including the pitot static system, transponder, ELT, ELT battery, VOR test, and GPS database updates (verify database cycle No. on the startup screen).

Date 20___	Pilot	Time			Destination/ Purpose
		Out	In	Total	

Total______

Squawks/ Inspections	Ok'd By	Date	Oil Added

Oil Change

Due:___________

100-hour

Due:___________

Annual

Due:___________

VOR check

Due:___________

Due:___________

Due:___________

Pitot-Static check

Due:___________

ELT check

Due:___________

GPS Database

Due:___________

Instructions: Describe any squawk affecting flight. Record the inspections you perform, including the pitot static system, transponder, ELT, ELT battery, VOR test, and GPS database updates (verify database cycle No. on the startup screen).

Date 20___	Pilot	Time			Destination/ Purpose
		Out	In	Total	

Total______

Squawks/ Inspections	Ok'd By	Date	Oil Added

Oil Change

Due:____________

100-hour

Due:____________

Annual

Due:____________

VOR check

Due:____________

Due:____________

Due:____________

Pitot-Static check

Due:____________

ELT check

Due:____________

GPS Database

Due:____________

Instructions: Describe any squawk affecting flight. Record the inspections you perform, including the pitot static system, transponder, ELT, ELT battery, VOR test, and GPS database updates (verify database cycle No. on the startup screen).

Date 20___	Pilot	Time			Destination/ Purpose
		Out	In	Total	

Total______

Squawks/ Inspections	Ok'd By	Date	Oil Added

Oil Change

Due:____________

100-hour

Due:____________

Annual

Due:____________

VOR check

Due:____________

Due:____________

Due:____________

Pitot-Static check

Due:____________

ELT check

Due:____________

GPS Database

Due:____________

Instructions: Describe any squawk affecting flight. Record the inspections you perform, including the pitot static system, transponder, ELT, ELT battery, VOR test, and GPS database updates (verify database cycle No. on the startup screen).

Date 20___	Pilot	Time			Destination/ Purpose
		Out	In	Total	

Total______

Squawks/ Inspections	Ok'd By	Date	Oil Added

Oil Change

Due:___________

100-hour

Due:___________

Annual

Due:___________

VOR check

Due:___________

Due:___________

Due:___________

Pitot-Static check

Due:___________

ELT check

Due:___________

GPS Database

Due:___________

Instructions: Describe any squawk affecting flight. Record the inspections you perform, including the pitot static system, transponder, ELT, ELT battery, VOR test, and GPS database updates (verify database cycle No. on the startup screen).

Date 20___	Pilot	Time			Destination/ Purpose
		Out	In	Total	

Total______

Squawks/ Inspections	Ok'd By	Date	Oil Added

Oil Change

Due:____________

100-hour

Due:____________

Annual

Due:____________

VOR check

Due:____________

Due:____________

Due:____________

Pitot-Static check

Due:____________

ELT check

Due:____________

GPS Database

Due:____________

Instructions: Describe any squawk affecting flight. Record the inspections you perform, including the pitot static system, transponder, ELT, ELT battery, VOR test, and GPS database updates (verify database cycle No. on the startup screen).

Date 20___	Pilot	Time			Destination/ Purpose
		Out	In	Total	

Total______

Squawks/ Inspections	Ok'd By	Date	Oil Added

Oil Change

Due:____________

100-hour

Due:____________

Annual

Due:____________

VOR check

Due:____________

Due:____________

Due:____________

Pitot-Static check

Due:____________

ELT check

Due:____________

GPS Database

Due:____________

Instructions: Describe any squawk affecting flight. Record the inspections you perform, including the pitot static system, transponder, ELT, ELT battery, VOR test, and GPS database updates (verify database cycle No. on the startup screen).

Date 20___	Pilot	Time			Destination/ Purpose
		Out	In	Total	

Total______

Squawks/ Inspections	Ok'd By	Date	Oil Added

Oil Change

Due:__________

100-hour

Due:__________

Annual

Due:__________

VOR check

Due:__________

Due:__________

Due:__________

Pitot-Static check

Due:__________

ELT check

Due:__________

GPS Database

Due:__________

Instructions: Describe any squawk affecting flight. Record the inspections you perform, including the pitot static system, transponder, ELT, ELT battery, VOR test, and GPS database updates (verify database cycle No. on the startup screen).